MOTHERHOOD FOR TRUTHFUL WOMEN

SALLY BRENDEN

Table of Contents

This helpful treatise on the feminine condition is dedicated with great love and affection to the New Generation of Nelson Women:

> *My delightful daughter, Stefanie*
>
> *My future daughter-in-law should she come to be*
>
> *My nieces: Amy, Katie, Molly, Bethany, Sarah, Alyssa and Haley*
>
> *And to nieces who join our family by marriage*

INTRODUCTION

Not all that many decades ago, I left my professional job and became a stay-at-home Mommy for six years during what I call "Lambing Season". My son, Matt, was two years old at the time. Chad was added two years later and Stefanie two years after that, with my returning to the professional world part-time when Stefanie was two.

I went from excellence in managing people and millions of dollars to the baffling world of wee ones, one of whom would be diagnosed with autism. Added to the twist was my husband working evenings so I did a lot of "single parenting".

I was a loving Mommy but I was an absolute "flop" at everything else related to "homemaking".

What is a mother to do?

The way I saw it, I had two options: one was to laugh and pray; the other was to lament and beat myself up.

I chose to embrace my deficiencies and in so doing, discovered a strange but noble calling – that of making other women feel normal, nay superior.

Lambing Season is over for me, but perhaps yours is just beginning or you find yourself in the thick of the fray. I hope that these stories, written during rare moments of tranquility during my Lambing Season, will help you realize that any woman who acts as though she and her kids are perfect is lying through her teeth. And any woman who throws away her one crazy wonderful life on keeping her house spotless, should have her head examined.

Hang on for dear life! Pray like everything depends on it (which it does)! Celebrate your imperfections, for there is no way they can be as bad as mine.

By the way, I think you're a great Mom just as you are! Take my words for it.

Chapter 1

Housekeeping Hints from a Hovel

It was the best advice my mother ever gave me.

"Give visitors an eye full the first time they come and after that nothing will shock them!"

I don't have an argument with cleaning in general. As a matter of fact, I even believe in spring cleaning. In the spring I scour, disinfect, fumigate and sandblast. No mold, sludge or dry rot is off limits.

What I object to is continual cleaning that is to no avail: like scrubbing the kitchen floor. With three preschoolers on the loose in another few months it needs to be scrubbed again.

For too long I was intimidated by Mr. and Ms. Clean who kept me on a constant guilt trip. Never mind that I was utterly exhausted from caring for three mini-tornados. I tried everything imaginable: hiding when company came, hanging "Anthrax Quarantine" signs, and using twenty watt light bulbs and letting people in only during low light.

Enough is enough.

I'm ready to do battle with those cleanliness freaks. Cleanliness is not next to godliness. It is next to impossible.

1

I'm fed up with those articles on cleaning tips. Who dreams up all those absurd hints? Pray tell what kind of a mind reels throughout the night determining that soy sauce and sheep placentas will get crayon marks off the wallpaper? Or that eggplant marmalade will remove car rust? Would you believe eye of newt?

I used to fall for promises like "$9.99 Robot Can Clean Your Bathroom in Five Seconds". I even ordered one and the only thing it cleaned out in five seconds was my wallet. Now I put all those scams on the caliber of "I Gave up My Life as a Public Relations Executive and Became a Christmas Tree".

Sure I believe in a clean house. I also believe in the four headed chicken from Mars with the IQ of 350 who gave birth to an albino alligator.

Part of the problem is that you need assistance from the rest of the family to keep the house clean. However hard I try, I still cannot trick my kids into believing it's more fun to scrub the bathroom than to go fishing. And while my husband keeps the garage organized and his boat immaculate, equality in our marriage has not extended to use of indoor cleaning products.

When I want to hide anything from my family, I just put it next to the dish soap. It can backfire, however, as recently I hid some money there and didn't find it myself for a month.

Call us legion for we terrible housekeepers are many. It's about time someone came up with some suggestions that actually work.

Let me offer a few that work for me.

<u>When You Do Clean, Go All Out</u>. Even if it does cost one hundred dollars a day, I rent that backhoe.

<u>Find Creative Ways to Get Your Family Involved</u>. I know of no normal child who will volunteer to scrub the bathtub, but she will if she needs it clean enough for her snakes. Let your toddler be responsible for cleaning the carpet. I haven't vacuumed in eight years and our kids score off the charts in small motor coordination.

<u>Find Ways to Eliminate Unnecessary Work</u>. Never stack dirty dishes

or you'll have to wash both sides. Permit only house pets that don't shed.

Look for the Positive in Filth. Every home needs a message center. The dust on the coffee table is just one possibility. Dirty windows make it easier for the kids to concentrate on homework. Or use filmy windows to record the growth of each child. Each of our children has his own window and from year to year we marvel at the changes in their handprints.

Set Firm Rules. When my kids come home from church in clean clothes, they know that they are free to play outside without changing, but if they plan to play in the house, they must change into something grubby.

And if you are ever caught off guard when company comes, do as we do.

Entertain in the garage.

Chapter 2

How to Get Your Man to Help With the Housework

The story is all too familiar.

Before our marriage my husband was an immaculate housekeeper. Perhaps it was because he had only six items to keep clean: a card table and two folding chairs, a mattress, lamp and alarm clock.

Perhaps it was because he didn't have a husband messing up everything. Inside his freezer, TV dinners were neatly stacked, one for each day of the week.

On one surprise visit I found him on his hands and knees cleaning the bathroom stool with a toothbrush.

I could only gloat over my good fortune.

Now there are creatures twice the size of a toothbrush running around the bathroom.

What happened to Mr. Tidy? I have never been able to relocate him and it's not for lack of trying.

I'm not asking for the world. Just maybe he could make the bed when he gets up last.

"I used to make my bed in the military," he says.

So, when there is no threat of court martial does a man lose his motivation to keep his surroundings clean?

Say what you will about the military, but you can't argue that they know the secret for motivating a man to cleanliness.

Nagging, badgering or threatening is of little avail. You tell me: am I blowing things out of proportion?

Why should I mind tripping over his shoes in the middle of the living room when I stagger out to nurse the baby at 3 a.m.?

Is it asking too much of a man who lifts weights to maximize upper body strength to carry the milk carton to the refrigerator when he's done drinking out of it?

Do physical therapists have proof that he's more likely to strain his back picking up his sox than netting a forty pound musky?

I'm open to scientific evidence and arguments that will hold up in a court of law. But no flimsy excuses.

Advice from marriage experts isn't worth a hill of beans. I have never been particularly impressed with the use of rewards. Like, promise him a new boat if he cleans his whiskers out of the sink? Threats are equally ineffective as he weighs twice as much as I do and I can't beat him up.

I've often pondered, how DO you get through to an intelligent, loving man that you need domestic assistance?

While I still have a way to go, I have learned some things in fifteen years of marriage that may help you if you are in such a quandary.

DISPEL MYTHS. Dishes do not wash themselves. Similarly, babies do not change themselves. Hot soapy water is no harder on hands than dipping fingers into the freezing water of a minnow bucket while ice fishing. Food does not appear by magic in the pantry; someone has to buy it. The same is true of milk. And it is no harder to pick towels off the floor than to pick up a bowling ball.

START WITH THE BASICS AND BE SPECIFIC. Be sure he knows what you're talking about. Start with a tour of your home. Identify the rooms he is unfamiliar with. Explain that the table can be cleaned after eating by putting dirty dishes in a place called the kitchen sink. Tell him the large object next to the sink is called a refrigerator and that is where he can put the milk. Inform him that the microwave he uses to make popcorn can be expanded in usage to heat other edible food stuffs should he feel led to get involved in meal preparation.

TEACH PRINCIPLES AND CONCEPTS. Explain the purpose of a broom, a mop, a vacuum cleaner. Astound him with the fact that small appliances are plugged into outlets just like power tools. That a drill and a hand mixer are very similar may have never entered his mind. Show him how washing windows on your home is like washing windows on his sports car. The same is true of polishing furniture and waxing his boat. Help him see that a rotary beater functions much like a fishing reel and that, similarly, changing a roll of toilet paper is like putting new line on one of his fifty fishing reels.

SPEAK HIS LANGUAGE. "There is a device called a vacuum cleaner that looks something like a golf cart and sounds like second gear of your motorcycle." Other helpful suggestions include:

*   "This dishwasher is like a giant tackle box".

*   "Loading a washer and dryer is like shooting hoops." (You may find it helpful to draw a net over them to make it more realistic.)

*   "The bathtub is like your Winchester. You clean it every time you use it."

*   "Pretend the dishcloth is a chamois."

*   "Please pick up a limit of milk."

*   "I need you to check the vacuum cleaner. Something is lodged in the chamber."

RECOGNIZE YOUR LIMITATIONS. There are allergies and phobias unique to men. Many men have allergies to dish soap, laundry detergent and household cleaning products. Oven and glass cleaner and bathroom lime-away are especially caustic to tender male skin. Men are more frequently injured by bathroom plungers, scrub brushes and feather dusters than by rifles, motorcycles or speed boats.

Phobias of small appliances like can openers, blenders and mixers are common. Irons have been known to paralyze many a man. Electrical shock can occur should they ever attempt to lift a toaster to clean crumbs. Appliancelargophobia, a paralyzing fear of large appliances such as stoves, refrigerators, dish washers, trash compactors, washers and dryers cannot be overcome without professional help. What is so mystifying about this severe psychological disorder is that the fear does not extend to the TV, VCR or sound systems.

DON'T CRITICIZE THEIR EFFORTS. Criticism will negate all the aforementioned good advice. As long as your man gets involved in housework let him do it in his own unique, perhaps frightening, way.

In fact, go beyond acquiescence and encourage his feeble efforts.

Every Christmas I get my husband a new kitchen shovel.

Chapter 3

Family Portrait: Lives out of Focus

It shouldn't be all that difficult to get a family portrait taken for a Christmas card.

Theoretically.

Year after year we get Christmas pictures of beaming and beautiful families decked out in Sunday finery looking healthy, happy and reasonably bright.

It makes me sick.

"Maybe we ought to get a family portrait taken for our Christmas card this year," I say to Mr. Wonderful, seeing as how we don't have so much as a Brownie snapshot of all five of us.

So Project: Family Portrait was undertaken.

It was a good thing we began early.

Thinking it'd be fun to get our picture taken in our natural setting we contacted a freelance photographer. But when he saw our natural setting he declined the job. I wouldn't think of letting out any pictures taken inside our house, and there isn't much for posing with in our yard. Most of the elms are long dead, the yard looks like the heart of the Sahara, and even Prince Charming couldn't cut through our hedge in one hundred years. The utility shed would be the most likely prospect for a backdrop had a tornado not taken the roof back in the 40's.

So we just made an appointment to go to Penney's. That way we'd have enough warning so we could look our best.

Again, theoretically.

Deciding what to wear wasn't a snap. The kids not only insisted on choosing their own garish outfits but also brought along their favorite props. Even the photographer had said it was best to look natural though she later recanted.

Matthew, our athletically inclined son, held his roller blades and helmet, baseball glove, hockey stick, soccer pads, goggles and snorkel. It looked a bit much but at least it covered up some of his outfit and his sister's latest attempt at cutting his hair.

Chad, not to be outdone, brought a colander to wear on his head and Daddy's old leech bucket filled with his belt and tie collection. At the last minute he couldn't find his Big Bird bedroom slippers so had to settle for a pair of Daddy's hunting waders.

Stefanie needed only her "blankie" which, perhaps not surprisingly, is what is left after two years of a discarded oversized ladies foundation garment, origin unknown.

To put it mildly, the portraits weren't exactly flattering. Realistic, yes; flattering, no. We looked like a poster family for a genetic counseling center.

Proof # 1: Mr. Wonderful looks like he'd overdosed on a black listed drug and I look like my third lobotomy wasn't particularly successful. The photographer thought it was quite a coincidence that all three kids' noses were running at the same time and since only Matt was wearing long sleeves, Chad is pulling up my skirt to use the hemline as a hankie.

Proof # 2: We're all grinning and look like a before picture on an orthodontist's wall. The last time we all smiled at the same time was when the health inspector determined we were only partially to blame for the city-wide lice infestation. My hair looks like it was cut at the Toro dealer and the furry object Stefanie is holding is what remains of the gerbil that had been missing since Easter. Leavings from Mr. Wonderful's last goose hunting trip are clearly visible on the bottom of Chad's waders and Stefanie's "blankie" is caught in Matt's snorkel.

Proof # 3: There are four people. When Matt's hockey stick hit Chad in the back of the head it knocked him off the platform and he's not back in the pictures until proof # 6 when he regained consciousness. My bifocals are askew on the one good bow, the result of Stefanie elbowing me to maintain her balance when Chad bit her prior to being hit in the head by the aforementioned hockey stick. Luckily I was wearing the black jock strap to hold my glasses up. The electrician's tape holding the bridge together makes a pleasant contrast with the toilet paper swatch Mr. Wonderful forgot to take off his chin when he nicked himself shaving the week before.

Proof # 4 is a close up and a sad testimonial to the fact that we've never heard of soap or toothpaste, let alone a comb or an iron. Our expressions look like we are witnessing a hanging. Or, to put it more honestly, that we are closer than witnesses. My shingles and Matt's festering facial sores show up worse than on the other proofs although Stefanie's left eye, swollen shut from a sty, minimizes her severe cross eyes.

Proof # 5, a full body shot, is no improvement. I am wearing one scuffed saddle shoe and one spike heel which in the commotion to look our best I never noticed. Mr. Wonderful can't say anything as the zipper is busted in the fly of his canary yellow polyester leisure suit. Stefanie is holding up her skirt. Which would be cute had she not left her undies in the Rambler.

The other proofs weren't as good.

And you think your driver's license picture is ugly.

I'm not laying the blame on the photographer. She isn't a miracle worker. Unfortunately. It's not easy making a group like the Barker family look good.

Project: Family Portrait was not a rousing success but we're still sending out a Christmas picture.

I went to Walmart and found a beautiful family of five and bought fifty pictures. Heaven knows what we'll do with all those frames, but at least until they see us again, every recipient will be impressed.

hapter 4

Sew What? A Christmas Fabrication

It was Stefanie's first Christmas. A beautiful black velvet dress trimmed with white lace in the display window of Baby Boutique caught my eye. It would be beautiful on my little red-haired angel but the price tag was outrageous.

The lady pushing the next cart of screaming kids remarked knowingly, "Isn't it highway robbery what they charge for kids clothes? You can make a dress like that for next to nothing."

She was right of course. I could make a dress like that. There couldn't be that much to it. I'd made an apron in 7th grade Home Ec and had pulled off a D+. Surely after twenty five years I was ready to tackle another sewing project.

Shortly thereafter I found myself in the foreign territory of a fabric store.

"A pattern," I said to myself, "I start with a pattern." Two hours later I'd narrowed it down to two, neither of which resembled the dress at Baby Boutique.

Feeling quite accomplished I headed for the cloth. (I was to learn later that it's now called fabric or material.) The variety made me want to

13

bolt. Some I could eliminate immediately. Upholstery remnants sounded too rough for tender skin. Surge was a milking machine when I lived on the farm. Crepes you eat. Forget damask. I didn't want a fabric she would wear only at Halloween. And lawn! You've got to be kidding. Not the way ours looks.

Most of the fabric I'd never heard of: challis, pindots, peau de soile, cotton belle, deluxe acetate twill. It got worse: charmeuse, tissue faille, boucle, modal, ramie, and barathea.

A kindly salesperson jolted me out of my stupor and led me to the velvet. But she thought black was too somber for a baby so I switched to blue.

"Would you like some ribbing?" she inquired. "No," I quickly responded. "I'm sure I'll get plenty of that after the garment is made."

We stopped at the thread. "Do you want mercerized cotton, polyester or nylon?"

Perhaps I looked somewhat blank because she went on. "Polyester comes in cotton wrapped and long fiber. For nylon, you can choose between monofilament, lightweight and woolly."

"I'll take the cotton," I said, "Blue cotton."

"Do you prefer firmament blue, cielo blue, soldier blue or parakeet blue?" There were twenty two additional shades of blue.

"Don't you have just blue?" I pleaded.

She looked at me like I was ordering vanilla ice cream at Baskin Robbins. But she found blue.

I was sure I could choose rick rack and a zipper without assistance. How wrong I was.

In the rick rack section I found maxi piping, twill tape, soutache braid, bias tape and hem facing and they all looked like rick rack to me.

Choosing a zipper was no easier. There were nylon and polyester, closed bottoms, separating and reversible zippers, and of every conceivable length.

I made a spur of the moment switch to buttons. They should be easy to choose. Wrong again. There were twelve million different colors and sizes.

I signaled the salesperson.

It was time to interject a little humor.

"I can't seem to locate the star shaped ones with the quilted baboons."

"Do you prefer pilot blue, baltic blue or dark teal?" she immediately responded.

"Do you have all the notions you need?" she asked innocently. Believe me, lady, I thought, I have plenty of notions and not a single one of them is hanging on your wall.

Honesty and desperation compelled me to stop momentarily at the sewing aids. Several looked helpful—fabric cement and a glue gun. Somehow I forced myself to pass up the bodkins and the horsehair braid.

"What type of machine do you have?" inquired the salesperson warily.

"I don't have a machine," I admitted. "I'll be doing this by hand."

"Have you done much hand sewing?" she queried. "Not recently," I answered evasively, quite sure my D+ apron experience would not impress her.

Surprisingly she didn't seem shocked and directed my attention to a $5 basic sewing kit and a $13 book on sewing essentials that informed me that no person was truly equipped for hand sewing without beeswax and a see through T-square.

I was also shown a $30 sewing basket which I quickly declined. I had a match box at home that would work just fine.

Not wishing to appear unappreciative for all her help, I said, "Since it's been a while since I've sewn (like one quarter of a century) maybe you could tell me what types of seams and stitches I should use."

Obviously a skilled seamstress, she knowingly advised, "It'd be cute with mock flat-fell or welt seams. Just use your whip stitch with a herringbone or half-back stitch on the bodice."

She paused. Somehow she knew I didn't have a clue what she was talking about.

"You aren't familiar with those are you." It was a statement not a question.

"No, Ma'am," I confessed.

"Do you think you could manage a prick stitch or a blind stitch?" she asked. "Quite easily, I think," I assured her.

She totaled up my purchases in silence. My face turned ashen at the amount on the cash register.

"I'm terribly sorry," I muttered embarrassingly, "but I'll have to make a withdrawal from my savings to cover this."

The kindly salesperson smiled knowingly and said, "Are you sure you really want to make this outfit? I saw a darling black velvet dress at Baby Boutique that you might be interested in."

Was I ever interested!!

And Stefanie looked like an angel in her store-bought black velvet Christmas dress.

Chapter 5

And I Thought the Miss America Pageant Was Depressing

I didn't think anything could be more depressing for a haggard woman over forty than to watch a stage full of talented young lovelies compete in the Miss America pageant.

I was wrong; there is something far more depressing.

It's watching a stage full of stunningly beautiful, poised, talented, articulate and intelligent married women my age compete in the Mrs. America pageant.

I tried to trick myself into believing that it was possible for young unmarried women with beautiful bodies and nothing by time on their hands to depress the dickens out of a frumpy matron like myself. But when I see married women my age putting those young ladies to shame I have a full blown depression on my hands.

These women in the Mrs. America pageant not only could make Miss Universe look like a dog; they do so while maintaining demanding careers like CEO's of Fortune 500 companies. They are on the Board of Directors of all manner of impressive charitable organizations and still find time to be raising children who will one day be president, if not the pope. And since they can function on two hours of sleep they still find time to model for Vogue and train for the New York Marathon.

Women of this caliber shouldn't be Mrs. America. They should be canonized.

The contestants are undeniably gorgeous. That in itself doesn't depress me, even if the only man who ever called me foxy was missing both his teeth and his rightful mind. I can even tolerate their stunning bodies in skimpy swimwear although the only way I'd parade for millions in mine is by covering up with a pair of my husband's waders. I suspect these women do not represent a cross-section of the nation's multigravidas.

And all that dancing and fancy choreography! I can barely walk without bumping into inanimate objects, let alone prance around on a slippery stage in four inch heels.

But what really depresses me is the talent competition. These women make Yo-Yo Ma look like a novice.

I'd love to compete for Mrs. America. But even assuming a miracle could be wrought with my appearance and body, a feat no less spectacular than the parting of the Red Sea, I wouldn't have a prayer in the talent competition.

You be the judge. These are my finest talents of which to boast:

Making toast

Licking stamps

Modeling support hose

I do have other less impressive gifts. Picture me telling millions of viewers, "Now I will drink a cup of coffee."

How about if I recited my grocery list or demonstrated how to camouflage bathroom dry rot?

Let me tantalize you further. I could put away two banana splits in 30 seconds or share tips on how to keep leeches and other live bait from smelling up your refrigerator.

Digging deeper into my latent storehouse of gifts, I could imitate the sound of three kids screaming simultaneously or show how quickly I can fall asleep.

You're not impressed? Ditto for the judges.

But I still haven't given up that someday there will be an obscure pageant created that I can enter, nay snag the crown.

It would be just such a shame for the world to miss out on my talent.

Chapter 6

Crafting With Lint and Other Ways to Make Millions at Home

Let me make it clear up front that I have no personal quarrel with women who are clever enough to make a grand a day working out of their homes.

But I don't think that many of us women who want to be home with our kids and yet still contribute to lowering of the family debt have any idea how we can get a piece of that action.

We cannot move an already lucrative legal, medical or business practice into our brownstone. The ads promising big bucks working from our homes, even if in compliance with vice laws, are highly exaggerated to put it kindly. And many of us have no hobbies or skills that seem remotely marketable.

Being a member of the latter group, I have found surprisingly, it is not only possible, but easy to make money at home—if you're willing to be innovative.

Develop a specialty. Don't copy someone else. Be original and find your niche, however frightening that may be. Specialize in selling either a service or a product. Since I am more of a service oriented person, this is the route I usually go. Presently I tutor other mothers getting their diplomas through Owl Correspondence School and provide meals-on-wheels to fishing widows. During the summer since I already have the hedge clippers sharpened, I give reduced rate hair-cuts and manicures—offering a group rate when pets are included.

I'm convinced that anyone can make a product that will sell. One trip to a craft sale will prove nothing is too far out to sell to some gullible soul. Although I am not a crafty person, I have a corner on the local market selling lint Christmas ornaments.

I also have contracted with trap ranges to sell my homemade biscuits for target shooting in lieu of expensive clay pigeons.

<u>Do something others will not do for themselves.</u> That's why sewer cleaners and vermin exterminators have such a racket going.

Just an ad on the bulletin board at our local supermarket has brought me more work than I can handle in wood tick removal. As a family we do Poop Scoop detail at parades which not only generates income but provides exercise and a unique vantage point from which to view the parade.

My next venture, when I need the money badly enough, will be a twenty four/seven flu clean-up service.

<u>Get paid for something you're already doing.</u> This is the key to being a wise entrepreneur. I contract with research departments at universities to be a guinea pig and have been well paid for many interesting and meaningful projects including studies on:

-sleep deprivation

-life cycles of rabid bats in dank basements

-average number of hair follicles turning grey daily

-frequency with which slugs on a sofa move

A cursory glance at our yard shows income possibilities. We board goats during the summer for vacationing shepherds. We don't even have to advertise; our lawn is its own advertisement. We've had farm-ers stop, too, asking if they can bale the clover in the front yard. Not only do we make money, we feel good knowing we've helped the heart of America stay solvent another year. We rent the back yard to an experimental station or just put it into the Soil Bank program.

Let children help bring in money. Our kids have thought of very ingenious, albeit bizarre, ways to make money. Selling used toilet paper rolls door-to-door to gerbil owners not only pays for their school clothes, but gets them out of the house. While this is not a concern of ours, theoretically it could also pay for their college education.

By following these few simple principles you will be able to kiss employment out of the house goodbye. (You may also have to kiss your dignity goodbye.)

You'll be amazed at how much money there is just waiting to be made at home.

And keep your video camera handy. There's not a day that a normal (well, that may be a bit of a stretch) family doesn't have enough bizarre happenings to win $10,000 on "America's Funniest Home Videos"—certainly a profitable day's work for anyone wishing to work at home.

Chapter 7

Prerequisites for Motherhood

"I just know I'll be a terrible mother," lamented my friend, a first-time mother-to-be.

She was right of course. She had absolutely no qualifications for motherhood.

When will women begin to realize that there are some minimum requirements to be met before the stork pays a call?

I've been there. I can tell you exactly what expertise you need before becoming a mother.

* Prisoner of war: Mothers go months (many of us, years) without sleep. You must be able to function semi-intelligently on three interrupted hours of sleep a night.

* Monk: You face celibacy from utter physical exhaustion. You will see no action for months.

* Shepherd: Spending time with sheep will get you used to smelling like Hogan's goat. Throw away your Chanel Number 5. From now on it's Eau de Baby Spittle.

* Farmer: Manure removal is now on your job description and

there are no machines to make the task more pleasant. I grew up on a farm where there wasn't any high fallutin' equipment and we pitched dung by hand so I was prepared for this malodorous task.

*   Diplomat: Your children will embarrass you to tears every chance they get. You must think quickly when they insult strangers. When my son was two and a half he saw a very rotund woman in a crowded public place. "Look, Mom! She's obese!!!" he shouted. That was not an easy one to worm my way out of.

*   Security Guard: Children snitch forbidden objects. You must know how to pounce on them before they take a chunk out of the middle of the cake on its way to the church potluck. I, however, can't really blame my kids for trying to sample the few items produced in my kitchen that are edible.

*   Weight lifter: Mega-strength is required to carry two kids, three bags of groceries, twenty overdue library books, a diaper bag and your purse at the same time with your good arm or to move large appliances single-handedly to extricate wedged children.

*   Drill sergeant: The ability to frighten children into obedience when courtesy, logic, cajoling or direct orders fail (like most of the time) is mandatory.

*   Miss America: You must be stunningly gorgeous so after sleep, no makeup, and monthly showers you don't get asked by some small cherub as was my mother, "Lady, are you a witch?"

*   Professional wrestling referee: While I am hardly a fan of professional wrestling, I must admit I am awed by the referees who are able to break up the brawls of giant imbeciles. Although no one would question that breaking up toddler squabbles are infinitely more difficult, a referee background would give you an idea where to begin.

*   Buzzard: You will never get to enjoy food again. Chairs to sit on and tables to eat at are not something that mothers use. All food and beverages will be consumed at room temperature,

ice cream included. Of course you only get leftovers and you must be hungry enough that even stale and spoiled food tastes good.

* Siamese twin: Mothers are never alone for a second. You will not use the bathroom alone until your children are in college. Or prison.

* Medical school graduate: If you haven't gone to medical school how will you know how to pry play dough out of little ears and noses or which spiders are edible? And you won't know after which regularly served meals to induce vomiting.

* Savant: You must have the uncanny aptitude to remember whose turn it is for every conceivable activity under the sun. The rest of your intellectual functioning disappears. Mothers are the only people who can legitimately plan their own surprise party or hide their own Easter baskets.

A word of caution: Don't get too discouraged if you don't meet all the requirements initially. And don't spend a fortune buying books and magazines telling you how to parent.

All you really need to know is that kids are miniature wild animals.

The best preparation for motherhood is spending lots of time at the zoo.

Chapter 8

Getting in Shape

"Now that you're forty you really ought to get in shape," suggested my cocky little doctor, just before I pasted the twerp to the wall.

He messed with the wrong Mama.

Who says I'm out of shape? I have more shapes than you can shake a stick at.

Okay, so my body isn't in perfect condition. Maybe I'm slightly out of sync with those weight charts the insurance companies use. Maybe way more than slightly. And yes, of course, I don't like little kids blindfolding me and hitting me with a stick hoping candy will fall out.

But I'm not alone.

There are six billion people on this planet. Only five hundred exercise regularly and every last one of them has their own morning exercise shows or exercise videos.

Have you noticed how all those self-appointed health gurus have all the answers? Anyone can change. You can be anything you wish to be. Just think positively. I think positively they should take a flying leap back to La La Land.

They get scientific, too, dividing us into body types that mean absolutely nothing even to members of MENSA. They entice you by

29

throwing out names like Raquel Welch, Princess Di, Sophia Loren and Elizabeth Taylor, as though no matter what body type you possess you can still awe millions with your enviable physique.

How can dowdy matrons like me relate to such hogwash? Is there any way we can make the most of what we don't have?

In the ignoble words of my esteemed Scandinavian ancestors, "You betcha!"

Just use a little common sense, an ingredient they seem to be sadly lacking.

Dieting is a hoax.

If it wasn't for the money generated by diet books our economy would be in even worse condition. There are no less than twelve million diet books at every public library. A representative sample includes The Nathan B. Hale Tucumcari Squid Diet and The No Flab Amino Acid Diet for Cobblers and Other Self-Employed Artisans.

Forget dieting and concentrate on learning the fundamentals of nutrition:

* Failure to get the minimum daily requirement of chocolate causes rickets.

* Six or more cups of black coffee daily will stimulate estrogen production and prevent osteoporosis.

* Pastries are the best source of iron.

Some women put a visual reminder on their refrigerator door to help them eat more sensibly. I have found a picture of a herd of grazing elephants to be helpful.

Diets are not necessary if you just learn to cut back. Only order one banana split at the Dairy Queen. And try smaller portions. Start cutting pies into quarters.

Be realistic about your own body.

Who gives a rip if you wore a size eight wedding dress? After three kids, size twenty four is not out of line.

Accept yourself as you are now. If you feel you need exercise, don't wait until you're in perfect shape to join the female fitness sickos in spandex. I feel ridiculous prancing around in tight leotards but perfectly at home in a class of sumo wrestlers.

Exercising is okay if tailored to your hectic lifestyle.

Here are some suitable possibilities:

* Facial stretches—Hollering at the kids keeps facial muscles taut and inhibits aging.

* Tongue extensions—Stick out your tongue at your kids when they do it first.

* Shoulder shrugs—Copy the movement of your children when you ask, "Which one of you broke the patio door?"

* Deep breathing—Mothers hold their breath half of the time. Like when they see the two year old on the roof.

* Fist flexes—Self-explanatory and automatic.

* Armpit power—Put knuckles under your pits and practice a Tarzan yell "SSSSUUUUPPPPPPPPPPEEEERRRRRRRR" to summon kids home from neighboring villages.

* Back breaks—-Carry sleeping teenagers to their own beds.

* Sit ups—-Get in and out of bed ten times a night to check babies, fetch drinks, potty children.

* Warm up stretches—-Dislodge children from underneath beds when they hide to escape detection.

* Leg lifts—-Place least swollen foot beneath bottom of child seated two inches from TV. Move in increments of one foot until child is at safe distance from screen. (A fun variation on this exercise is giving kids and their father rides on your feet.)

Whatever you do, don't neglect the most important exercise of all:

31

body curls. Five extra minutes in bed every chance you get will work wonders.

Take it from me. I'm a horse to be reckoned with.

Chapter 9

Earth to Women: Betty Crocker is a Figment of Someone's Imagination

When I got married I received several cookbooks. I used them for bookends.

Six months later, after the doctor put my husband on an ulcer diet, I decided I should crack open the cookbooks and try to unravel the hidden secrets that had so long eluded me.

I totally panicked.

For the next fifteen years I broke out in a cold sweat whenever I tried to read a recipe. It's not that I hadn't been involved in food preparation since my youth. Why even before I was able to read, Mom made me memorize a recipe for Happy Day cake which I made every time she needed a yellow cake.

I'd always blamed my recipe phobia on my childhood. Everything was made from scratch; recipes were passed on by oral tradition. We never seemed to have all the ingredients the humblest of recipes called for so there was little point in following written directions.

It had always bothered me that I, a person generously labeled dull normal, had a recipe phobia.

But then I made an amazing discovery.

There was nothing wrong with *me*!

The problem was with the recipes. The recipes you see in cookbooks and magazines are unreasonable and unintelligible.

Consider some of their assumptions.

1. You don't have kids.

Never read recipes included in sample menus. It's too depressing. Now I know what a terrible mother I am. If I really cared about my kids, I'd serve this menu for supper tonight:

Brie Bisque with Baguette Croutons

Shrimp Ratatouille Loaf

Mediterranean Mahimahi

Dill Chapati

And

Mosaic Fruit Terrine

Mine are lucky if I let them loose under the table to clean up scraps from lunch or if I add a fresh layer of peanut butter and jelly to their cheeks. I take some consolation in knowing that for special occasions I do cook things they really like such as bubble gum hotdish and chocolate chip Jell-O.

2. You're a millionaire.

How many of us struggling to feed our families on a reasonable or meager budget can afford the ingredients? I do not include pomegranate molasses, fermented tofu and iberico ham on my biweekly grocery list on a regular basis and although there are lots of capers at our house, none are edible.

There is probably about as much variety in my pantry as there was in those of the pioneer women after a long winter. And although it has been a source of shame for many years, I confess I grew up in a home where refrigerated angel-hair pasta and anchovy fillets were not considered staples.

3. You have a peaceful environment and endless time to prepare exotic meals for your family.

Magazines use catchy titles (lies, I call them) to make you believe such a feat is possible such as "Ten Nutritious and Inexpensive Meals to Make in Less Than Twenty Minutes".

Baloney!

I'm sure your supper hour when you're supposed to whip out these meals is no different than mine.

I'm standing at the stove nursing the baby and stirring the chocolate pudding so it doesn't scorch when the cheese on the frozen pizza in the oven spills on the heating element, sending smoke billowing and setting off the smoke alarm. The three year old, momentarily distracted from coloring on the living room wall, dashes in and grabs my legs, screaming hysterically to be held. The seven year old, just hit in the nose by a bat, is wiping the blood on the back of my shirt when the phone rings and a vacuum cleaner salesperson thrills me with the exciting news that I've won a carpet demonstration.

And my husband, busy polishing his boat, calls, "Is supper ready, honey?"

See what I mean? Those Betty Crocker clones make assumptions that have no connection with reality.

Once I realized that my aversion to recipes was rational, I developed my own guidelines for recipe selection. Now before I consider any recipe I ask myself six questions.

1. <u>Have I heard of all the ingredients?</u> For all I know fusilli could be some spore formation. Belgian endive or crème de cassis could be nuclear contaminants or pesticides. I don't know a baba from bechamal. And quahog sounds like a fat pig.

35

2. <u>Do I have all the necessary ingredients or suitable substitutes?</u> Mostly I make substitutions. When a recipe calls for crushed saffron threads, I use salt; if it calls for marjoram sprigs, I use pepper. Sugar is my choice when I'm fresh out of crystallized ginger. And if I don't have a suitable substitute, in the case of packed arugula leaves and pignoli nuts, I just leave them out.

3. <u>Can I understand the cooking instructions?</u> I'm not an idiot; I passed 7th grade Home Ed. (well, the cooking part, at least). But I found studying Greek much less of a challenge than deciphering Recipese.

For the life of me I cannot understand why recipes call for cannelli when they can use modern English and say white kidney beans. (Not that I have any idea what they are either.) And how sheltered of a life I must have led to make it almost to forty without knowing that orzo is rice shaped pasta.

Who do they think understands their recipes? I was thirty five before I figured out when someone said to use a "tisp" it meant a teaspoon.

I'm reasonably adept at draining, combining and adding. Then I find out I should know how to rice, stud, dredge and acidulate. Sometimes I can figure out only half of the directions as in the case of melting fat and flour to make a roux. And when I was young, blanch was a neighbor woman.

4. <u>Do I have the necessary cooking equipment?</u> While even my own mother says I have the fewest cooking utensils she's ever seen, (I don't believe in clutter), I have the basic equipment: a knife, a wooden spoon, an incomplete set of measuring cups. I even have an egg separator that I won at the only Tupperware party I ever attended so it's not like I haven't heard of fancy utensils.

But get a load of what you are expected to own: slotted spoons, pastry blenders (I'm assuming they are not referring to my fingers), Hobart mixers and number 8 star tubes. The worst is a Dutch oven. Can you believe the nerve? I'm not about to go out and buy a brand new stove when my old GE works perfectly fine.

5. <u>Is it best served at room temperature?</u> Nothing is served warm at my house except ice cream. And that is either with or without the nesselrode.

6. <u>Will inanimate objects complement the texture?</u> It is difficult to totally eliminate foreign objects from food. Flying projectiles from fighting siblings, grey hair, building blocks, refrigerator magnets, fishing sinkers and small coins have a way of becoming part of our dining delights. If this will detract from the food, the recipe is eliminated from consideration.

Now that I have a system for making wise choices, my phobia is finally gone. I'm no longer afraid of recipes. As a matter of fact, I just might write my own cookbook.

There has to be a market for <u>The Totaled Woman Cookbook</u>.

Chapter 10

Marriage Incompatibility

How often I have heard women moan, "My husband and I are incompatible." Like since when is that some revelation? He's a man; you're a woman. Of course you're incompatible.

It goes much deeper than he likes crunchy peanut butter and you like creamy or he likes to sleep with the window shut and you like it open.

There are deep, and I mean deep, differences.

So start with the most obvious: sexual.

To say that men and women are sexually aroused differently is an understatement. Let a lady with a shapely pair of legs and an amply endowed bosom saunter past and a man will salivate as surely as one of Pavlov's dogs.

Not so with women. Our libido skyrockets when a man does the supper dishes and puts the kids to bed. Men often lament the lack of romantic action and yet never see the connection between chronic fatigue and women's lack of desire in the boudoir. A woman's idea of a sexy man (at least after we become mothers) has nothing to do with a full head of hair and a slim physique. It has everything to do with backrubs, Sunday afternoon naps and days off.

Another difference between men and women is their noise level. Women are quiet. We lay stiff as a poker in bed not moving a muscle, stifling sneezes and foregoing urgent trips to the biffy lest we rouse the baby who has finally fallen asleep.

Men are noisy. They toss, turn, flail and snore at a decibel level that could wake the dead two states away let alone a fitfully slumbering baby in the next room.

When they leave at 4 a.m. to go fishing they open and close the garage door ten times to make sure everyone is up at that ghastly hour and when they return at 11 p.m. the same scenario is repeated, once again waking up all just-barely-sleeping children.

Getting ready to go to work in the morning is no better. Linen closets, medicine cabinets, kitchen cupboards and refrigerator doors slam endless times. The john is flushed so often you wonder if he has some gastronomical malfunction. Showers run long enough for him to warble both sides of a Randy Travis tape. The radio is cranked up to be heard over the hair dryer and the smoke alarm pierces the thick of the fray when, in his one attempt at feeding himself, the toast burns. Then, making sure to scrape the chair on the floor, he sits down to breakfast, amazed that everyone is up to see him off to work.

This is the same man who can sit in a deer stand without making a peep for thirty hours straight.

Men have less acute senses than women. They can't hear babies cry between the hours of 10 p.m. and 6 a.m. In fact they have difficulty hearing kids' noises any time of day. A man can watch TV or sleep on the couch while the kids engage in violence which could lead to a manslaughter conviction—and not hear a thing. One is truly baffled that he can distinguish between the call of a Canada goose and a bluebill at one half mile.

A man can't see a thing in the dark so the whole house is illuminated when he gets up during the night lest he stub his toe on the shoes he left in the middle of the floor. It would never occur to him to shut the kids' bedroom doors instead of blinding them with the sudden influx of 300 watt bulbs.

Women, on the other hand, can do anything in the dark. We take kids temperatures, change diapers, prepare bottles, mop up barf and can even differentiate between black and navy sox in pitch dark. We also have the presence of mind to take things we'll need out of our closet the night before so we don't have to storm into the bedroom and wake up our mate at the crack of dawn looking for our underwear.

A man's sense of smell is different. Diaper doo makes him gag. Yet he can fillet fish, clean goose entrails, gut a deer and maintain a vertical position in the stench of a locker room.

A man is not built to work with lightweight objects. He has no trouble lifting barbells, car motors, or blue marlin fish, but replacing toilet paper rolls and pulling up bed sheets has caused many a hernia.

The ghost of Houdini lurks within a man and he is capable of mystifying disappearing acts when children are to be dressed for church or to be bathed.

A man thinks only in terms of black and white. Women are creative. We know how to substitute and make do with what's available. Case in point: our volleyball net broke and our son came in to report the sad news.

Daddy's response: We'll buy a new one, Son.

Mama's response: Stretch out a pair of my undies and you'll have a regulation sized net.

I have no sympathy for any woman bellyaching because she and her husband are incompatible. Where has she been all her life? Any woman with the brains to blow her nose should have known that before she invested that hard-earned fifty spot in a marriage license.

Of course she and her man are incompatible. And that's half the fun.

Chapter 11

Lies Women Tell: An Expose´ of Christmas Letters

I was intrigued by the ease with which women lie even before my elderly aunt received Honorable Mention in the Burlington Liars Contest.

For most of us it is with greatest vigilance and deep self-abasement that we tell the brutal truth.

It defies diagnosis how women who are sincerely trying to raise honest and upright young citizens can tell tall tales that would make Paul Bunyan stories seem tame.

Case in point: Christmas letters.

What do women find to lie about in these yearly atrocities? Simply everything! Starting with their kids!

> "Victoria Elizabeth was invited to the Senior Prom by her steady. She'll miss the Junior Olympic tryouts in France but maybe in two years when she's in sixth grade. She didn't want to miss the Prom as it's only the third year she's been invited.
>
> We were pleased that Maximilian was tentatively accepted into Harvard. He's the only one in his nursery school who's been accepted so far. He is a natural leader and has already been put in

charge of passing out straws at snack time. He has learned Portuguese, Swahili and Arabic on his flash cards and his tuba teacher says he shows unbelievable talent for a one year old.

Windsor was captain of his football, baseball and soccer teams and was All-State in five sports. He played the lead in the school musical, was president of the Student Council and editor of the school paper. Last summer he was elected president of Boys Nation and traveled abroad in a fifteen member symphonic orchestra with the other best violinists in the world. As he's maintained a 4.0 since kindergarten most of his classes are independent study through Oxford. Sometimes it's hard for him to relate to kids his age. Of course, with his looks and charm that's' certainly not true with the girls.

Being a parent of children who find it so easy to excel has its challenges!"

My kids present vastly different challenges and it takes me considerably less space to write about them.

Matt's third year of second grade seems to be going better. He is learning the three primary colors. He just got his driver's license but prefers riding his sister's Big Wheel to driving our spare garbage truck.

Chad was allowed back into school after missing most of last year for disciplinary problems. The time off gave him a chance for his permanent teeth to come in.

The principal advised us to give Stefanie a little longer to mature before she starts kindergarten. We were reluctant to hold her back but he assured us that she wouldn't be the only fifteen year old in her class.

Women also stretch the truth about the men in their lives.

"Pierre was promoted again this year and is now CEO of the Trump Empire. We hate all the international travel and being away from the kids so much. Along with his many community activities he personally raised nine million for his Yale alumni Association. Everyone wants him to run for the Senate next fall."

Big deal! I had an uncle in the House of Representatives. He was the elevator operator.

I can write about my Better Half, too.

> Homer was laid off most of the year. We were thrilled that at least he wasn't fired this time. Neither of us knows the meaning of the word promotion. Or raise.

Vacations get their share of grandiosity.

> "We went to Marrakesh this year. Hong Kong gets old after a while and how many times can you go to Tahiti or the Great Barrier Reef?"

I'm really not sure. The farthest I got this year was to the mailbox and that was only during nice weather when the front door wasn't frozen shut.

It nauseates me to hear about their yachts, homes, cars and fancy possessions.

Let me tell you just what is new at our house. I turned 300,000 miles on our '65 Nash in August. It's a piece of junk but we can't afford a newer car until we get it paid for.

We have our house up for sale. It was appraised at $11,500 prior to being condemned. We hope it sells as we have our eye on one with electricity.

These women always collect antiques. So do I but for vastly different reasons. If I had the money to buy something for the house, we'd love indoor plumbing.

They brag about going to fancy spas and getting expensive perms at elite salons with current magazines.

I don't need that. I'm always in hot water and just being a mother makes my hair curl.

> "The President and First Lady were here for a BBQ en route to Camp David."

We had one visitor this year, too. In June the county protection worker visited us to conduct a pre-sentence investigation.

They never tell the truth about their age, their figure or their appearance. I can appreciate that. It takes guts to admit the last time I was with Grandma someone asked if we were sisters.

It's easier to discuss lofty goals that will never come to fruition. She plans to go back to college after the kids are in school. She is entering pre-law or pre-med (always some pre-supposedly-impressive major), never pre-tallow making or pre-vermin extermination technician that doesn't hold the same ability to inspire awe. In the meantime she stays busy with her volunteer work which she embellishes ad nauseam.

Not me. If I ever do get my kids in school, I'm going on a well-deserved ten year coffee break.

And when I divulge my scant volunteer involvement, I'm brutally honest. I re-tape the <u>Spot Takes a Walk</u> books for the public library and sort pocket gopher feet for the county agricultural agent.

But after years of resisting I finally got on the bandwagon with all the prevaricators and began writing a Christmas letter, too.

And it's wonderful!

It's the only time of the year I can tell the sorry truth and no one believes a word of it.

Chapter 12

How a Dirty House Enhances Your Child's Creativity

It has been scientifically proven that you can triple your child's creativity just by keeping your house comfortably dirty.

How sad it is that there are so many well-meaning parents living in ignorance, believing that a clean environment will contribute to the likelihood that their child will be another Einstein. Actually, cleanliness is detrimental and stifles both creativity and intellectual growth.

Every child psychologist knows the value of free play in a sand pile. Ours is in the living room next to the piano. We also have provided each of our children with his own spacious garden plot to grow fresh produce year around: behind the refrigerator, under the playpen and in between the stereo speakers. Instead of giving your children an allowance, let them learn money management by raising cash crops. Drought is never a problem with toddlers freely watering with apple juice.

To encourage scientific discovery keep a microscope handy for examining the many interesting organisms indigenous to your home such as amoebae, black larvae and South American spiders.

Your home is its own craft store. Art supplies are bountiful. Hardened macaroni and cheese (spiral and wheels are always favorites) make decorative wall plaques. Also popular are milk soaked cheerios that have dried and are stuck to the floor. Little round sausages from frozen pizzas are an eye catching addition. Frame with petrified bread crusts spread with peanut butter.

Gum dried in carpeting can be used instead of expensive play dough. You have a variety of colors always at hand and if it ends up in little mouths you don't have to call the Poison Control Center.

Let your child make his own gifts to give as birthday or holiday gifts. Take two Ritz crackers from under the microwave cart. Stick them together with syrup that never made it to last week's pancakes. In between, wind the used dental floss lying next to the bathroom wastebasket and you have a delightful yoyo that any youngster would be proud to own.

Are you looking for new ways to get your child away from the TV or VCR and get some exercise? Dust balls have endless safe and fun uses. Injuries are seldom and never serious. Your child's motor coordination will also be challenged when every room he plays in is an obstacle course.

While my kids' favorite dust ball is a medicine ball, they are also wonderful for basketball, soccer and football. If you catch them early enough, they can be used for ping pong or golf. For a game of indoor golf that even the adults can enjoy, pick up a discarded breadstick and putt away.

How about starting some festive holiday traditions? At Christmas, send the children on a scavenger hunt to locate popcorn from under the sofa and easy chair cushions. Last year mine found enough to not only cover our tree, but also to decorate the national Christmas tree well into the twenty-first century.

Have you given up on indoor Easter egg hunts? We almost did as it was too hard for the kids to identify which eggs were just hidden and which had been buried in recessed spots all year. Now we are trying to salvage the tradition by using rocks covered in Reynolds Wrap, which should give the kids almost an even chance.

All children enjoy making their own jingle money. Let them catch the night crawlers west of the bathtub to sell to passing anglers who won't question where the kids got them. Or let them sell fresh mushrooms. We've found they thrive in the window sills and bedroom closets as well as the dark moist places behind the counter appliances.

As your child begins to take advantage of his surroundings and you thrill at the creativity you see developing, you'll be appalled to think that at one time you actually believed that the sterile environment of a clean home was the best place to raise a curious child.

Chapter 13

My Husband's Illness is Making Me Sick

My husband just had belly button surgery. I thought it was going to kill me.

You know how men are when they get sick.

Now I'm not singling out the strapping young buck I'm married to. I'm talking about men in general. It must be something in their genetic makeup because it's so universal.

Being a veteran of numerous surgeries, the most recent just a month before my husband's, it's not like I don't know what he's going through. He's healthy as a horse. To give you an idea just how familiar he is with hospital protocol, he tied his hospital gown in the front.

"Think of the bright side, dear," I said before he went under the knife, quoting what he had so recently told me, "At least you'll get away from the kids for a day."

As he convalesces I am putting Florence Nightingale to shame. Day and night I'm on constant medical alert, dashing in at the slightest tinkle of the little dinner bell he uses to summon me. But I must admit my thoughts are not always as charitable as my actions.

"I feel a little nauseated." Until you have kept up a mother's unbroken pace for five months while green with morning sickness or wretched bile during childbirth, don't bellyache about a little nausea.

"The kids are jumping on the bed." Only on the bed? When I had surgery they jumped on my incisions.

"I can't sleep." How could you when you slept eighteen hours yesterday and then took a three hour nap? The only way you'll sleep tonight is if I induce it by clubbing you with a five pound venison sausage.

"A backrub would feel awfully good." No doubt. I'll never forget that sixty second one you gave me back in the Kennedy Administration.

"This bed gives me a backache." Oh, sweet prince, maybe there is a pea under your mattress. Let me trade places with you for three uninterrupted hours just one night and I'll suffer with that terrible back pain.

"I don't want to go to my checkup. It's embarrassing to strip to my underwear." Come again? From a man who flashes me from the boudoir every time the kids have their heads turned? And to a woman who has had five hundred pelvics, three babies and fifty mammograms?

"A little exercise might help me get my strength back." (This in reference to an invitation to go fishing.) If you're looking for exercise, there's three kids to feed, change, clothe; dishes to wash; a house to clean; fights to arbitrate; beds to make; clothes to wash; dust bunnies to dispose of; garbage to haul ad nauseam. Need I say more?

"I can't lift anything for six weeks." One week after being told the same thing I was lifting seven loads of filthy laundry, twelve bags of groceries and fifty five pound kids. I must give him credit for helping lift one side of the piano to fish out the two year old who had fallen behind it.

"My scar looks terrible". Tell me about it. My body is so full of scars you can find the Big Dipper on my chest alone. Funny that it doesn't bother you to have that six inch scar on your wrist from the removal of a ganglion that interfered with your bowling.

"What's for supper?" It's between senegalese groundnut stew, armenian meat pockets and greek antipasto with eggplant dip. Or would you like me to just whip up one of our old standbys like cumin rice and black beans or polenta with walnuts? And for dessert would you prefer lemon schaum torte or papaya mousse flambé?

"A piece of caramel pecan silk supreme pie would taste awfully good now that I'm getting my appetite back." Like which job should I skip to find the time to make this succulent delicacy: sodding the yard, painting the house, overhauling your outboard motor, cutting down the dead trees, or roofing the house?

"Boy, I'd trade places with anybody right about now. I wouldn't wish this on anybody." You're looking at a willing volunteer. Wish it on me. Please. Wish it on me.

You get the picture. Moan. Moan. Moan.

Why can't sick men concentrate on all they can still do? The only restriction on my husband is that he can't lift more than fifteen pounds which still leaves a reasonable amount of work that he can do.

* Like the dishes for instance. There is not one dish or kettle in our kitchen that weighs over fifteen pounds. I know, because I weighed them all on his fish scale just to be sure.

* He can carry the sugar bowl back to the cupboard, lift out the toaster himself and fetch a twelve ounce can of pop.

* Theoretically he can carry his own pillow and bedding to the sofa on his daily pilgrimage to the living room.

* He can get our twenty pound daughter out of the crib by lifting one end at a time. He can also change any diaper weighing less than fifteen pounds.

* He can still participate in child rearing tasks. No, he can't lift. But the doctor didn't say he couldn't shove, drag or pull.

* Light housecleaning tasks can be attempted. Brooms and bathroom bowl brushes are lightweight and a feather duster just makes it under his maximum lifting weight.

53

I don't even want to mention how expensive this surgery was. No, we have excellent insurance and every cent was paid.

It's the incidentals that add up. Like the two new fishing videos he ordered (cost thirty dollars each) for the express purpose of "getting me through surgery" to add to the fifty other fishing videos he already has in his video library. Not to speak of every fishing magazine under the sun, which incidentally, they do not give away.

Of course there were the constant movie rentals. How else do you watch TV eighteen hours a day?

I must not forget snacks. Tell me, do chocolate malts really replenish blood loss? Will deluxe supreme pizzas minimize the risk of post-surgical infections?

It goes without saying we need to replace the couch. And the remote control for the TV is shot.

But the biggest single expenditure is a ten thousand dollar boat that he believes he has earned for all his suffering.

Yes, life is no "covered basket" living with a sick man. Lucky for me, the fishing opener is only a week away.

I sense a miraculous recovery is just around the corner.

Chapter 14

Hooked on Harlequins

I used to hide them in the bottom of the book bag under the Richard Scarry books. I was afraid someone I knew would see me coming out of the library with my stack of Harlequin romance novels. Why would someone who was of reasonable intelligence and sound mind before the onset of motherhood read such mindless babble?

For the same reason we got a kick out of fairy tales when we were kids.

Fantasy. Pure fantasy. There's something in every woman that yearns to be swept off her feet by a handsome man in a Lamborghini.

It doesn't bother me a bit that all the plots are identical. A beautiful young lady with a perfect body, perfect skin and a name so melodic that she has never had to resort to using an alias falls head over heels for a rich, handsome, sexy older man.

He wines and dines her at all manner of ritzy restaurants on food I've never heard of let alone tasted.

They attend beautiful concerts, plays and operas. The only opera I've ever seen is "There's Never Ever Any Trouble in Bubbleland" on Mister Rogers and with all due respect to Chef Brockett and Handyman Negri, they just don't have the vocal range of Pavarotti or Domingo. And concerts in the school gym featuring less than child protégées playing woodwind specialties like Dissonance in E Flat

Major somehow lack the ambiance of a Mozart sonata in a Vienna concert hall.

The beautiful maiden travels to exotic locations with greenery names you couldn't begin to spell in a game of Scrabble. In forty years I've only been out of the county once and that was to secure emergency medical treatment.

I drool when I read of the palatial homes with servants at her beck and call. She never shares a scuzzy bathroom with seven other people or has a crib squeezed into the master bedroom cubicle because there is no room in the attic bedroom the other six kids share.

Her eyes are limpid pools of turquoise or ebony, never bloodshot from chronic fatigue or hay fever. I've never met a Harlequin heroine with 20/200 vision or one who has to wash her silken locks in a tar-based psoriasis shampoo. If her body isn't totally perfect it's that her legs are too long or she's a tad too buxom for her 22" waistline. It absolutely breaks your heart.

There's a time for those of us with bulging cellulite and varicose veins to engage in harmless fantasy.

She is never entirely brilliant. She always waits until it's almost too late to catch Hr. Hunk. If she had any brains she'd grab the sucker and run by page twenty.

My favorite is all the description of her clothes. She looks ravishing in every color. Obviously she is every season. And she just happens to have some otherworldly designer dress with a deep plunging neck-line and diaphanous folds that cling in all the right places handy for that special occasion.

I wonder what she look like if she put on the rags in my closet. She never runs around in faded bib overalls splotched with paint or is still wearing maternity clothes when the baby is in college because she couldn't shed that last fifty.

And her lingerie and negligees are straight out of Victoria's Secret. My snazziest nocturnal get-up to turn on my man is my down thermal underwear from Eddie Bauer. They must turn the heat up to ninety degrees in those fancy houses so she can stay warm in those flimsy outfits.

And when they get to sleep after merrymaking half the night, there are no sick kids throwing up at 3 a.m., no preschoolers wetting the bed at 4 a.m., and no babies getting up for good at 5 a.m. If I could sleep till noon every day maybe I could catapult my husband to the heights of rapture, too.

Then again, maybe I couldn't.

I think what makes romance novels so fascinating is that is makes me think back to my single days when I wielded such power on all the men beating paths to my door. Not that I took advantage of him.

It's fun hallucinating back to the time when I had my youth, some sort of a figure, money to buy clothes at Walmart, and privacy for romance. Especially the privacy. Moonlit strolls around the lake, kissy face on secluded beaches, a canoe pulling ashore for a romantic picnic for two. Now Mr. Wonderful and I have as much privacy as the beluga whale exhibit at the zoo and you know how much romantic action they see in captivity.

I'd like to write a romance novel about my life, too, but people just would not feel it's titillating enough.

> She stood knee deep in the flooded basement, a vision in her chenille bathrobe and rubber waders. Her stubby fingers, nails chewed to the quick, were adroitly operating the sump pump as a rabid bat streaked past and lodge, unnoticed, somewhere in the recesses of her pink sponge curlers.

> The Earl of Seville stood a moment watching her. Transfixed. Nauseated. He spoke not a word but turned on the heel of his imported alligator shoes, rushed to his waiting limousine and was never spotted in Minnesota again.

People just don't want to read about reality.

The same goes for the racy parts.

> Selma lay in her rumpled house dress on the rollaway waiting for Einar, oblivious to the tormented sounds emanating from the horse

flies caught on the fly ribbon above her. Beads of perspiration from beheading and butchering twenty leghorns rolled off her pocked brow and followed a pinball course past her facial moles to her third chin.

Einar didn't even notice her when he came in from slopping the hogs three hours later. He ambled to the straight backed chair near the fan, tongued his plug of Right Cut further back in his cheek and without so much as removing his Pioneer seed corn cap or his manure caked work boots was soon snoring contentedly.

No wonder we prefer the tantalizing tales of romance.

If you find it unnecessary to occasionally retreat into the world of fantasy, more power to you. But the next time you sit down to broaden your mind with intellectually stimulating literature, think of me.

I'll be soaking in a bubble bath, lost in Forgotten Blonde Babe's Italian Holiday.

Chapter 15

I'm All Washed Up with Doing Laundry

The first time she did it, even I was slightly taken aback.

Instead of frolicking in the wading pool with Rubber Ducky, my two year old daughter took off her swimming suit, leaned precariously over the edge and began washing it in the water. She looked like our foremothers scrubbing their animal loincloths on the rocks.

Not wishing to discourage her feeble attempt at personal cleanliness or assistance with the family laundry, I let her wash not only her own clothes, but those of her beet-faced brothers.

Personally, I am all washed up with doing laundry. It's gotten so blame complicated. When I grew up we had a weekly wash day with the old wringer washer and then lugged twenty nine baskets of wet garments to the clothesline.

Now there are computerized washers and dryers costing nigh unto a grand a piece with programmed sound sensors and visual graphics showing tiny droplets to indicate how dry your laundry is.

Ridiculous! I'm not against modernization. I appreciate my washer and dryer six days a week when I drag hampers laden with grimy clothes to my dank and dismal underground laundry room. But who needs computers with twenty buttons for selecting five hundred different laundry options? I need two: dark and filthy.

I don't have the slightest idea which laundry products to use. There are zillions to choose from. The detergent options alone make me dizzy: powders and liquids, concentrated, heavy duty, stronger than dirt (wanna make a bet?), extra strength and triple action formulas. There are scented detergents and dermatologist tested detergents without irritation dyes or perfumes. They come with boosters, whiteners and brighteners, color safe bleaches and fabric softeners. To make sure your clothes get really clean, you can use spot lifters, stain sticks, sprays or stain removers designed specifically for baby stains, permapress or silk, wool and color fabrics.

And who thinks I have all day to follow their instructions? Wash darks separately. Phooey!! All I have is darks. It'd take a week a basket washing each dark separately.

Let me be the first to acknowledge that I'm an environmental stumbling block. I'm the only woman in the neighborhood who doesn't use her clothesline. And that's not only because it's in the way of the badminton net and I don't want my children to go the way of Absalom suspended in midair by their hair in the clothesline.

I only share the size of my unmentionables on a need-to-know basis, which at this point in time does not include the UPS man.

And even though I have a nodding acquaintance with the meter reader, it embarrasses me to have him pass the clothesline on Friday and see only my Monday undies hanging out to dry.

I don't feel that depriving my children hours of fun playing hide and seek in my billowing bloomers automatically makes me a terrible mother.

Perhaps the most honest reason I don't hang out my laundry is that I'm ashamed of how grungy everything looks. The neighbor's clothes look so white. My "whites" at best look like we live too close to Mount St. Helens. I'd only dare hang them out under the cover of darkness.

So I use my dryer.

I ruin a lot of clothes because I don't seem to be able to follow instructions.

"Lay flat to dry". Are you kidding? The only time I get to lay flat is when some kid pegs me unannounced from behind with a shoe and I don't have the time to first put on some wet garment to dry as I lie there.

Since I never sort the laundry it goes without saying that I dry everything at the same temperature. We do have some shrinkage problems but my four year old enjoys getting Daddy's only-worn-once shirts.

Wrinkle free products are a joke. Everything looks like Rip Van Winkle slept in it. Ironing has unnerved me ever since I scorched off the collar of my best silk blouse. "You should have used a cool iron," rebuked a friend. Hey, they didn't even have neon irons in those days.

It costs a fortune to keep everyone clean. You can have a lobster dinner at some swanky restaurant for what you have to sink into one trip to the Laundromat. The cost of doing it at home is not much less. Ours ranks right up there with our house payment.

I can tell you one thing. Now every time we go to the wading pool, I bring a whole basket of laundry for my daughter to wash.

Chapter 16

Hobbies, Fancies, Interests, Leisure Pursuits and Other Quests that Have No Relevance to an Exhausted Mother

"You don't have any hobbies?" gasped my new friend, as startled as if I'd admitted to assassinating the president.

"You'll end up wacko."

Maybe.

But surely I can't be the only person on the face of the earth who doesn't have a hobby.

To have hobbies you need talent. Money. Time. None of which I possess in abundance.

I have never been particularly successful at hobbies.

Perhaps the reason is that I always have tried normal hobbies and there has not been much of a fit. My cooking skill falls far short of gourmet, though I have not been accused of precipitating someone's demise as has my sainted mother.

I still suffer from flashbacks to 7th grade Home Ec. when I pierced my thumb on the sewing machine needle while making that blasted apron.

I was a failure at athletics. Even after working myself up to running a forty minute mile, my own kids clock me using a calendar.

And there is no negative number discovered that can accurately measure my mechanical aptitude and manual dexterity.

Then there is the problem of money. There's never been money for my hobbies; my husband spends all available shekels on his.

"But you spent $4,000 on yourself last year," he reminds me. "Yes, Babe," I admitted, "but that was on therapy to cope with your hobbies."

Then I became a mother and add to my lack of inherent ability and money the lack of time and privacy.

Some soul long devoid of a connection with reality suggested I get into jigsaw puzzles. Put a 25,000 piece puzzle of the sky on the coffee table and work on it as I have time. Get real! Are my three little kids going to leave it alone in the ten years it takes me to complete the border? Plus it's dangerous. Obviously the person who suggested this has never read Curious George Goes to the Hospital.

Other suggestions were equally stupid. Exercising, for instance. What do people think I do all day? Are dragging, shoving, pulling, forcing, swabbing and separating feats performed by an inert body?

Like a good mother I tried joining my kids in their hobbies but even scouring the neighborhood for fresh road kill and dislodging inanimate objects from auditory orifices lost its charm after a while.

Desperate for a hobby lest I fall into insanity as my new friend predicted, I devoured reams from the hobby shelves at the library.

The possibilities were endless. How would I ever narrow them down?

Making your own shoes

Creating egg carton lamp shades

Net making

Fun with wire

There was no end to the stimulating ideas:

Thatching a dovecoat

Making a zoetrope

Jacobean crewel work

Designing undies

After much deliberation I zeroed in on a hobby that seems perfectly suited to me.

I will make molas.

I don't have to tell a smart person like you that molas are colorful applique panels created by Cuna Indians who live in the San Blas territory of Panama. I figure that even if I'm no good at it (which, based upon my past experiences with hobbies, seems a distinct possibility), at least I won't have to put up with some smart aleck telling me that I'm doing it wrong.

My husband thinks my hobby is a bit peculiar and cautions me saying, "But darling, with a hobby like that people will think you're half nuts!"

Half?

Chapter 17

The Ugly Truth About Becoming Beautiful

I'm haunted by delusions of being one of those before and after pictures where a makeover changes me from a frazzled mother into a ravishing beauty; delusion being the operative word.

I can't quite place the origin of these delusions, as my experience to date certainly should not let me entertain false hope.

Feeling the need to make the most of what I didn't have, I had my colors "done". It cost me $950. The consultation only cost $50 but I had to fork over $900 for therapy to deal with the ensuing depression. I was anxious to learn my season. But I wasn't a season. I was one day: November 29.

It took a computer printout to list all the colors I should avoid. Every color from a box of 64 crayons was eliminated. So what was left? Muted federal indigo and King's Tavern pink, shades available only by special order in custom paint stores.

Every beauty book tells you to emphasize your good points. What they fail to mention is that first you have to find some. After painstaking scrutiny I came up with two: both of my eyes are the same color and the four most unsightly warts are on the same side of my nose meaning, theoretically, my face does have a good side.

With that amazing discovery and using an alias, I scheduled an appointment for a free consultation with a rep from one of those fancy cosmetic companies. I didn't want to expose myself to someone who might see me again. I was also influenced by medical wisdom, which dictates that there are instances when the intervention of a specialist is mandatory.

I had difficulty answering even the simple questions.

"What is your eye color?" Red was not even listed as a standard option.

"What is your natural hair color?" When it's just been washed or in the weeks in between?

"Does your skin have beige, rose or honey undertones?" Would you believe sallow and grey?

She lost me when she asked if I wanted the make-up for day or eveningwear. Come again? Who gets time to put on make-up during the day or does that include airborne baby cereal that I haven't had a chance to scrape off?

The only useful tidbits of information I left with were it wouldn't hurt my face if I washed it occasionally and the proper rest at night would do wonders to get rid of the bags under my eyes. Perhaps she'd like to explain that to my baby.

I avoid beauty magazines like the plague. I don't understand a word they say. For example I read that your powder should lightly dust your chin. Well, that's hardly specific enough. Which chin?

And all the hoopla about how the proper accessories can camouflage any beauty problem! I don't need to pay two bucks for a magazine to tell me what my brothers told me years ago: a scarf over my face would do wonders.

Sure it's easy for them to make it sound easy, sitting in their fancy offices on Madison Avenue looking like fashion plates. You read that garbage and even Miss America would feel like a dog.

They are as bad as those ridiculous machines in cosmetic departments that will make an analysis and tell you what products you can't live without.

Can you believe how far from reality they are? "Is your skin in the T-zone oily, normal or dry?" Never mind that I haven't a clue what a T-zone is; there's no listing for scaly.

"Are your nails more likely to flake or crack?" Neither, frankly. Mine are more likely to get caught in the car door.

And all the time you're standing there beet red hoping no one you know sees you, you just know the sucker is going to blow up from the pressure you're putting on it.

If I bought everything that blame machine suggested, it'd cost more than my husband's fishing tackle. Well, that's an exaggeration. But it would put you back a bundle.

What's so discouraging is that even after all my attempts to become beautiful, I still have absolutely no idea which products to buy.

So I stick to the one's I've always used—anything with words like concealer or mask.

And I buy without question any product containing the word miracle.

Chapter 18

My Name is Sally and I Have a Black Thumb

To say I don't have a green thumb is a gross understatement. Like saying the pope is generally Catholic.

Living greenery wilts and dies while I pass by.

A friend, no doubt thinking it was something we could enjoy for a long time, gave us a beautiful potted plant for a wedding gift. If our marriage ended as quickly as the plant we would have demanded a refund on our marriage license.

After living in a tiny apartment several years we bought a home. I was quite impressed with all the hooks the previous owner had placed on the ceiling to dry dishtowels until years later when my mother revealed that they were really for hanging plants.

The sorry truth is this: I have never had a plant survive.

Once I thought my luck had changed and one plant lived for six months. My husband caught me watering it one day and asked if there was any particular reason I felt the need to water an artificial plant.

We had a small garden plot when we moved into our home. My boss took sadistic pleasure in hackling me about my gardening ability. He'd come in the spring and till up the rocks so I'd have no excuse.

One year I almost got a crop. I'd planted six tomato plants and six green pepper plants. About midcrop I could make out one sickly pepper plant with one microscopic green pepper that had not been choked out by the thistles and brambles.

I got out the heavy-duty weed trimmer, determined to avenge my reputation as a hopeless gardener.

It was not to be. Just as I was about to cut through the root of the adjacent budding tree I cut my plant.

It was not long after that my husband incorporated my garden plot into the lawn. It is the only part of the yard that comes close to lush.

We seem to have an inordinate amount of difficulty getting anything to grow. The trees and shrubs perish the season they go in. And the only time we could possibly sell our home is in the dead of winter when ten feet of snow hide the sad condition of our lawn.

It doesn't make any sense. I grew up on a farm and if my dad had been as terrible at making things grow as I am I would have starved in infancy.

One summer, desiring to make a million and with no other prospects in sight to attain such a feat, my siblings and I decided to "raise pickles". In those days, companies bought cucumbers to make into pickles. We kids had something like one half of an acre of cukes. Now the key to making money is to find the cukes when they are little. Tiny cukes that could be made into baby-sized pickles received premium dollar.

We had trouble spotting them until they were giant orange and half rotten which the companies tossed into the reject baskets and only Uncle Ralph would buy a small amount for fifty cents or a buck to make into some sweet pickles he fancied.

Our venture was a complete disaster. My share for the entire summer was less than ten bucks and we never even paid Mom for the gas for her thirty-mile daily trip to Cucumber Control.

Over the years I have sought help from friends, fellow pedestrians, professionals and total strangers. I have come to the sorry conclusion that I just do not have a green thumb.

But that's okay. Some of us have to make the rest of you look good.

There's always hope for the next generation. One of my children shows promise of having a Green Thumb.

The Mother's Day pansy he potted in the living room carpet is growing beautifully.

Chapter 19

Shortcuts to Child Rearing

So you're another Super Mom? Well, I'm not. Never was; never will be. And if you face the brutal facts you probably aren't either.

Since no one can do it all, just what CAN a mother do? Only one thing: take shortcuts.

But where do you begin? Try my advice. I am a self-appointed expert.

ANTICIPATE.

Be ever vigilant for shortcuts that will work for your family and start when the kids are babies. Give everyone the same unisex hairstyle. One mixing bowl and a not-too-dull shears will get the job done. Line the kids up and chop away. No one will dare criticize how another looks. You may, however, wish to allow a store haircut for senior pictures.

Leave food within easy reach of children so they can get their own snacks and meals. A good cache under the sofa cushions is indispensable and will eliminate five hundred daily whines of "I'm hungry".

Cook in quantity and freeze leftovers. The way I cook there is nothing but leftovers. If there is a food you particularly like, give it a terrible name so the kids refuse to eat it. My husband and I call our favorite casserole "poison hotdish". The kids won't touch it and we feast for days.

75

COORDINATE.

Coordinate condiment usage with hair color. Blondes can use only mustard; redheads only ketchup. Our son with strawberry blonde hair gets to use either. Children with dark hair must be strictly forbidden to put sugar or salt in their hair lest a teacher suspect head lice and expects you to engage in mega-cleaning.

Coordinate kids clothing with menu for the day to camouflage spills and eliminate need for changing soiled garments. This is especially important with babies, toddlers and teenagers.

Be a schedule maker. Schedule bathing on a monthly basis. If you have four kids or less, it is a breeze. The first week of the month, child #1 gets a bath and hair wash; the second week, child #2. And so on down to #4. If you have more than four, go into the second month. If less than four, you or your spouse can take a turn or skip it all together and enjoy the free time.

ELIMINATE.

This is an art. Always be on the lookout for ways to cut back. Since laundry occupies so much of my time, I've had to find ways to cut back, yet keep my kids from being reported to the Board of Health. When weather permits, layer children with as many of their dirty clothes as possible, hose down after breakfast and let them air dry. Put towels and bedding on house pets and let them join in the fun. Separating laundry is not necessary. The way I do laundry, everything is dark anyway.

Don't get into the Super Mom complex of hauling kids to everything. Let each choose one thing that is meaningful and make sure the child gets there—school, the orthodontist, the therapist, a plumbing apprenticeship—and don't feel guilty about the rest. Let the children take responsibility for securing their own transportation to other events. We have found shoes to be a good investment.

Find creative ways to eliminate kitchen cleanup. Instead of cleaning the supper table, put a sheet over the table to pretend it's a tent and let the kids enjoy a camp breakfast. Rather than purchasing confining playpens, let babies and toddlers play under the kitchen table to assist in leftover removal.

DELEGATE.

Whenever possible let someone else do your dirty work. Let the dental hygienist clean your children's teeth. Ears can be cleaned by the pediatrician when checking for ear infections. College professors can teach them their alphabet and animal sounds. Their spouses will be highly motivated to assist in potty training.

DON'T WAIT.

Begin now. There are many shortcuts begging to be taken and both you and your child will benefit. Soon your biggest problem with child rearing will be deciding how to spend all your spare time.

Chapter 20

The Key to a Happy Marriage

With nearly one out of two marriages ending in divorce, when is someone going to tell newlyweds exactly what it takes to make their marriages work?

The secret to a healthy and happy marriage is quite simply this: never share your husband's hobbies.

Why no professionals have ever come forward with this simple truth is beyond me. Most are still advising couples to share interests if they want to stay together. I can tell you just the opposite is true. The reason my husband and I are still together is that long ago I quit sharing his hobbies.

Now I'm not averse to having some interests in common. Both of us are interested in bathing when it's warm, Hydrox blizzards, and letting the bathroom clean itself.

But don't make the mistake of participating in your husband's most important hobbies.

I married an avid outdoorsman with three hobbies: hunting, fishing, and planning (make that scheming) for hunting and fishing. You'd think I'd have questioned my compatibility with a person whose idea of fun was getting up at 3 a.m. to crawl on his belly through a muddy cornfield imitating the feeding chatter of a Canada goose.

I didn't question it, either, when, instead of an engagement ring, he took me to the bait store, bought a family fishing license and said, "Now *this* is a commitment!" (And I said, "You bet it is! I just owned up to within fifty pounds of my actual weight.")

First he took me goose hunting. I used a day of precious annual leave to get up at 3 a.m., stand in a shed reeking of cigar smoke and body odor to get our blind assignment (which was next to a parking lot), pranced for hours behind two hay bales to maintain circulation to my extremities and came home eighteen hours later with neither a goose nor a desire to ever go again.

"You'll like pheasant hunting better," my husband assured me. So he bought me a pair of unsightly green rubber boots and took me hunting. Although I think most people know the difference between a lady in green rubber boots and a rooster pheasant, one hunter apparently did not and I was shot.

And those were the good hunting trips.

Perhaps fishing would be more pleasant.

It was five hundred below zero on the walleye opener and again I was rustled out of bed before the crack of dawn and not so much as fed breakfast. The line, leeches and I all froze solid and I didn't get a nibble in the five hours it took me to convince my husband to drag me to shore.

I tried to make fishing more palatable by always taking along a seven course meal but the fact that it occupied the entire live well was a constant source of contention.

I did a lot of reading except for when a seven pound walleye had the audacity to bite and I couldn't shake it off. My philosophy was "If the fish start biting, it's time to move to another lake."

There were never bathrooms available and somehow I never fancied taking to the cover of a sumac patch. And although I yearn for three hour bubble baths, I never could get the same cheap thrill bobbing for hours looking through murky water at plankton and underwater vegetation.

I never refuse to cook his catches, though I am steadfast in refusing to eat much of it. If I have a hankering for seafood I feel safer with lobster than fresh walleye laden with PCB's that make my eyes luminous. And although we have tried every recipe known to modern civilization, my goose always tastes like one of Michael Jordan's tennis shoes.

It's been fifteen years since we entered the state of nuptial bliss. My husband's hobbies haven't changed. I didn't expect him to give them up. He simply found new partners.

Between his outings, we've managed to squeeze in several little additions to the family fishing license.

Chapter 21

Collecting Christmas Crafts: The Craze for Clutter

Ever since the Garden of Eden there's been crafty individuals with the beguiling ability to convince others they need something simply because they don't already have it.

Case in point: holiday craft bazaars.

Normally I don't venture near them, let alone cough up cold cash for any of their fancywork.

But this Christmas I set forth on a quest to gather the most absurd items available to give to my siblings who are equally abhorrent of meaningless handcrafted clutter.

Believe me, I was not let down.

For Mom, although I was sorely tempted by a 12 Days of Christmas padded thimble and a hen shaped egg cup with matching folded magazine napkins, I chose three toilet paper roll wise men with ecru crocheted edging.

My sister, Bonnie, who collects regional jewelry, will love her washer and nut necklace. Her husband, JR, a pilot with one eye always on the weather, will be equally taken aback with his corn cob wind chimes.

I found a beaded frog tie for my pastor brother, Tom, who needs something dressy. For his wife, Liz, harried mother of two tiny ones, I selected something impractical yet festive: an egg carton peacock.

Newlyweds Tim and Michele were easy to buy for. They will be the proud new owners of a bride and groom candy dish made from a gallon bleach bottle. Buying for my brother, Roger, who delights in slinking on hot beaches, was a cinch, too. Some inspired artisan was selling a French salad dressing bottle (with the label still on) filled with colored sand.

Sister Meg will be thrilled with her tin can poinsettia and her hairnet flower holder can hold fresh flowers throughout the winter while her bulbs lie dormant beneath the winter snow. And my brother-in-law, Jay, exhausted after a long day of teaching, will soon be able to don his newspaper slippers and bask in the glow of his newspaper reading lamp.

For my nonmusical brother, Andy, who was considered an unsuitable candidate for band lessons after pouring water down his baritone, a crepe paper ocarina.

My personal favorite goes to my new sister, Dian a psychotherapist: five assorted nuts painstakingly painted as people with bifocals, warts and bald spots, and with the words "Sometimes I Think We're All Nuts".

You think?

You don't have to convince me there's a sucker born every minute. And I want a piece of the action.

Next year I'm holding my own Holiday Craft Bizarre.

Chapter 22

Fox Paws

I thought it was my little brother calling from California.

"Hi, Sweetheart", I gushed into Ma Bell.

A long pause ensued.

"Perhaps you were expecting another party," murmured the startled sixty five year old plumber I'd forgotten would be calling.

My most embarrassing moment? Hardly. Just another normal faux pas in the life of a person who has to call Directory Assistance to get her own phone number.

If I had the presence of mind to worry, I'd be very concerned about some of the outrageous things I do.

I remind myself of the two old ladies in the nursing home my mother overheard discussing the date.

"Is it today or tomorrow?" asked the first.

"I'm not sure," replied the second, "but I think it's yesterday."

When I went to my first church potluck I thought I was complying with the instructions in the bulletin. It said to bring two dishes to pass. So I brought a cake pan and a plate.

It's not like I haven't been on the plumbers end myself so I know there are others out in the ozone with me.

Like in the middle of an electrical fire the phone rang and some turkey wanted to know if we'd be interested in a new roof. "If you don't get off the phone this very second, we will," I assured him, "But we won't be buying it from you."

Or, when five days post C Section, home alone with a newborn, a two year old and a six year old, the phone again rang and a gentleman inquires, "Is this Leisure Island?"

Pray tell why on earth are some of us so prone to such random acts of stupidity?

There are two theories. They sound equally plausible to me. One theory holds that something doesn't quite click upstairs.

My brother-in-law, a third grade teacher, had tried all year to impress upon a student the need to double check his spelling before handing in his assignments. The kid was so appreciative he gave my brother-in-law a note on the last day of school: "Thak you for hepling me."

Another theory holds that it is genetic and this seems credible in that I see myself in my grandmother and my son.

Grandma, wishing to express her condolences to a granddaughter whose husband had died in a boating accident, purchased a sympathy card. The verse inside was "He leadeth me beside still waters."

I was going to visit an uncle who was gravely ill and thought it would cheer him up if my five-year-old drew him a picture to hang in the stark hospital room. Happy to oblige, Matthew drew a picture of a man in a coffin surrounded by beautiful floral arrangements.

Loved ones, concerned professionals, and anonymous passersby have tried to come to my aid and offered many suggestions. "Slow down." "Think before you speak." "Count to ten before you speak."

And I try every suggestion.

It all helps.

Chapter 23

"Talk is Sheap"

As a child, I overheard the conversation of an old Swedish neighbor to my father. "Talk is sheap, Yoe, but it takes money to buy shicken wire."

Go figger!

But I did get the gist of the conversation. It is easy to offer advice.

A different neighbor, a sad faced elderly farmer with blood shot eyes, constantly offered unsolicited advice. His name was August. He never listened; he just spewed forth advice and opinions.

The world is full of Augusts. Folks only too happy to offer advice without any idea of what they are talking about. Everyone is quick to give advice, particularly on child rearing.

As a general rule, I don't give advice. Not because of my early encounter with August, but because I am seldom asked.

Some years back I saw an announcement for the Kudos Working Mother of the Year Awards. I believe the grand prize was something outrageous like $25,000, some large amount that would certainly have gone a long way to alleviate a working mother's financial woes. The prize was to be awarded for the best parenting tip(s). The limit was five hundred words.

The deadline was December 31. Unfortunately I read the announcement about a week before the deadline. While I'm not saying the outcome would have been different had I been allowed more time, I am assuming I wasn't selected since a goodly number have years have passed since I submitted my entry. Like twelve.

The contest rules, as I recall, asked the women to give their best parenting tips.

I did a lot of thinking in the short time allotted to me, and the tips identified in that aborted attempt at fast financial security hold fast yet today.

And so, I offer my serious advice on parenting.

Concentrate On Your Home, Not Your House

As a harried older working mother of three children equally distributed on the Bell curve, motherhood is no "covered basket." Literature, apart from the writings of early martyrs and saints, sheds little light on parenting. I suspect the majority of the nations' multiparas are desperate for advice that works.

Raising Children: There's A Lot To Be Said For Survival

* Always bring church candy.

* Never feel guilty pulling a fuse or circuit breaker to stop the TV.

* Most children will survive if they go to bed with dirty feet.

* "Catch them being good" is a crock. Rewarding behavior occurring yearly is not frequently enough to establish a habit.

* Put them to bed early on school nights.

* Put them to bed early on weekends.

* Let them make bubble gum hot dish and chocolate chip Jell-O.

* Never start "turns".

* Velcro will make your life easier.

* Let them eat green apples.

* Buy them flowers.

* Say "yes" often.

* Make them write thank you cards.

* Love their Daddy.

* Say grace.

* Let them see you cry.

* Take them all in your bed and snuggle them when it storms.

* Rock them in the dark when everyone else is sleeping (even when they're older).

* Play with them in the sand pile by moonlight.

* Turn up the car radio when they fight.

* Make them eat the same number of peas as their age.

* Wear the bag of M & M's they gave you for a Mother's Day corsage.

* Take them out of school and go fishing.

* Make tents in the living room.

* Let them snitch cookie dough.

* Make them keep one foot on the floor when reaching at the table.

* Wrap them in your robe and have cocoa together in the moonlight.

* Feed the ducks.

* Chase butterflies.

* Designate one day of the week as "Gripe Day".

* Take each one on a date weekly.

* Backrubs, prayer, and fellowship at the bus stop are more important than hot cereal.

* Enjoy "lambing season". Nurse your babies.

* Take them to funerals.

* Let them decorate their birthday cake.

* Buy lots of mittens.

* Bath time is for fun, not cleanliness.

* Teach them to minister to others.

* Choose your battles. If it's not important in light of eternity, it's not that important.

Don't Forget Yourself: Put Whipped Cream in Your Cocoa

* Forbid clutter.

* Go with cravings.

* Keep the cookie jar full of YOUR favorite cookies.

* Get braces at forty.

* Order often from Victoria's Secret.

* Leave your business card in your husband's car with an irresistible proposition.

* Make scales contraband.

* Ignore the doorbell.

* Cleanliness is not next to godliness; it is next to impossible.

* Enjoy your work.

* Celebrate the real meaning of holidays and skip the rest.

* Love your own brothers and sisters.

* Time alone to think, dream, meditate and pray is more important than sleep.

* Choose "the road less traveled".

* Model an unshakeable faith.

* MAKE YOUR HOME A HAVEN WITH A BLUE JEAN FEELING ON THE INSIDE.

Take my advice for what it's worth. Talk is still "sheap". And who knows if they even sell "shicken" wire anymore!

Thank you for carving out time to read my stories. Don't listen to the naysayers or braggarts. And don't be so sure the "experts" know more than you do. Pour a cup of coffee or hot chocolate, sit down, put up your feet and relax. Take your eyes off your work and listen to your heart. You are a gift to your family...and to the world.

Regards,

Sally Brenden

OTHER BOOKS BY AUTHOR

SLIGHTLY ASKEW
Stories for Your Heart

I serve as a warning to others.

It appears that I have been blessed with overactive stupid genes since I have been doing witless things pretty much since birth. And the sorry truth is that adulthood with its passages into career, marriage and parenthood has only added fuel to the flame.

Some experiences are so shockingly embarrassing, so totally mortifying, so absolutely foolhardy, so utterly harebrained, you really do have an obligation to humanity to share them.

So go ahead. Read. Behold. Laugh and mock.

(Like you're perfect?!)

GOD IN THE SERENDIPITY
Stories for Your Heart

While most of my life, and probably yours, is lived Under the Mystery, there are cherished moments of serendipity when the Creator of the Universe surprises and overwhelms me by entering my small world. I call these glorious times, God in the Serendipity.

Special moments and unexplainable experiences when God surprises me with an awareness of His presence, power, protection, love, even tasking me to conduct Royal Business in His behalf – life changing experiences where I know in my heart of hearts it is Him.

Does He enter the lives of ordinary people living ordinary lives? Are there moments when He is so present you have no doubt that it could only be Him or do you live out your days in this customer unfriendly world of ours not convinced He has shown up for your life?

Do I have stories to tell you!

TREASURES OF DARKNESS
Unwrapping the Gift of Autism

This is a story of a very special gift. It was not a gift I would have chosen; it was a gift God chose for me. And as you know, or perhaps will be given the heart to know, gifts that God hand selects are the best gifts you will ever receive, even though it often takes time to gain a heart of wisdom.

My Gift's name is Chad Timothy. He is my beloved son and he came wrapped in autism.

You may also have been given a glorious gift, though unrequested and with a "no return policy". Don't throw away the gift just because God's wrapping paper looks different.

Join me as, over a period of twenty six years, I unwrap my Gift from God. Perhaps it may give you courage to open yours.

AN HONORING DEATH
A Primer for Families

Join me, a novice to death, as I direct and record my sweet Mama's three week drama of death. Walk with our family through the gut wrenching natural death process dictated by her health care directive and learn how to apply this to your upcoming situations with love, unity, and faith. Project yourself into our true story and "try on" how your family could survive and thrive in a similar and inevitable crisis. Insightful and well established hospice and palliative care explanations are added by my sister, a palliative care nurse and hospice educator, who coached us from across the country.

From the honest and intimate pre-death conversations, to Mom's re-created dining room set and her autistic grandson leading the call to worship at the memorial service, you will gain creative ideas as well as be challenged to step out of the box and confidently weave your family experience into a uniquely honoring death for your loved one.

By the way, we saved 65% over average purchased funeral services.

BREADCRUMBS ALONG THE PATH OF LIFE

Hansel and Gretel would have been dead meat early on had not Hansel had the wisdom and foresight to sacrifice his measly piece of bread to leave breadcrumbs along the path so they could find their way home.

The woods of life are dark and deep. Dangers lurk; peril abounds. At times my heart races at near panic. How will I ever find my way out of this impenetrable and unending forest?

Chances are you've been lost, too. But take heart. Feel the panic subside. There is a full moon rising and if you look closely, you can make out breadcrumbs along your path.

I know these woods. Let me help you get you started on the path Home.

It would be an honor to have you visit us at
www.brendenbooks.com.

.

95

Made in the USA
San Bernardino, CA
15 April 2016